NATIONAL GEOGRAPHIC

T0069722

My Walk

Zoe Sharp

SUBURBAN
S
ATHLETICS

2 Bell Court

E EAST
L 4386
30

OPEN 7 DAYS
HOME DELIVERY
SUBURBAN
ATHLETICS

UPERMARKET
ideal dairy
SUPERMARKET
ATM
cash
Available Here
ATM
cash
Available Here
Streets
International
Roast
$5.00
Weekly Special
MIRACLE
$1.00
Weekly Special
Weekly Special
Potting Mix

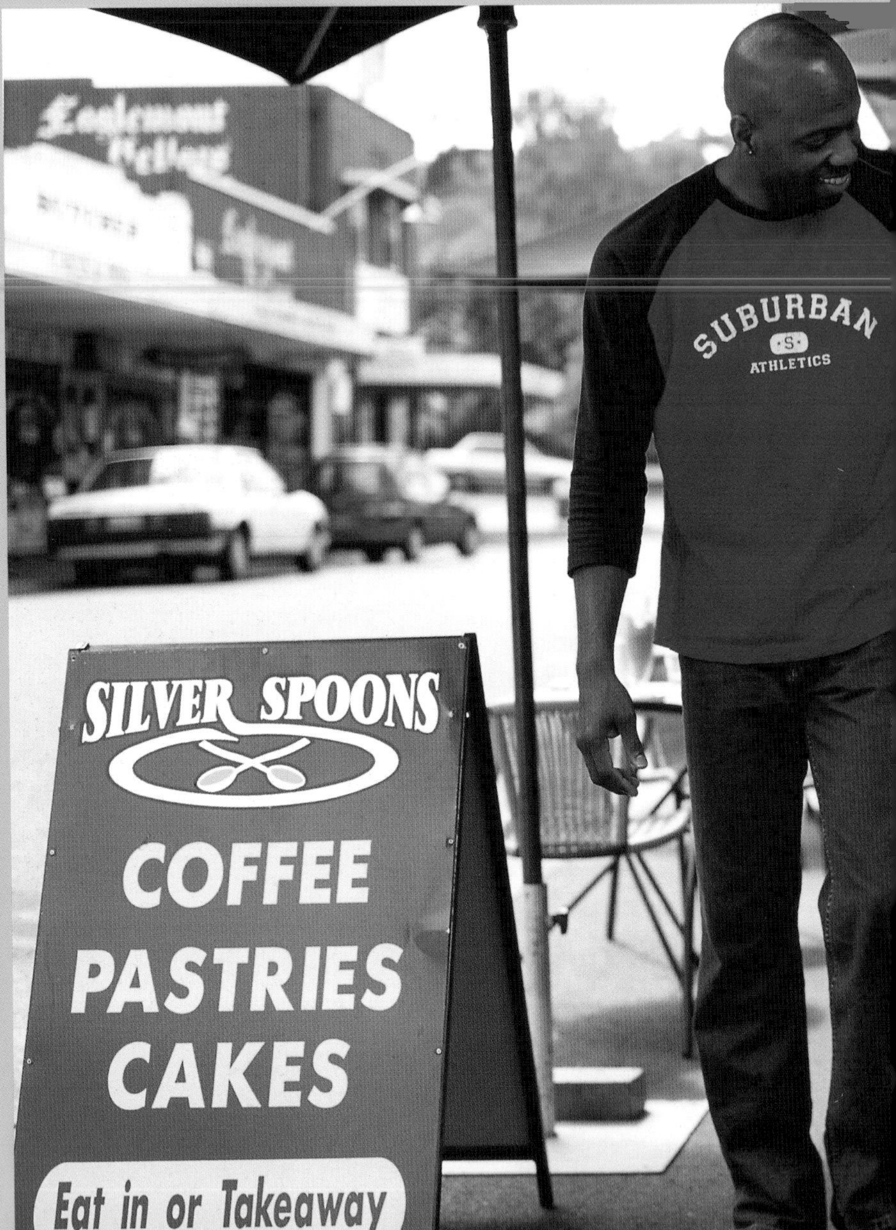
SILVER SPOONS
COFFEE
PASTRIES
CAKES
Eat in or Takeaway
SUBURBAN
S
ATHLETICS

POONS

Gifts
Better Homes and Gardens
FREE GOLD STARS
CHRISTMAS!

Photos
SUBURBAN
S
ATHLETICS

Animal
Hospital
IVANHOE
VETERINARY
CLI
SURGEON

15

SUBURBAN
S
ATHLETICS